Tulsa Art Deco Experience

The Art Deco style of architecture is an integral part of the Tulsa landscape. Art Deco was a design style most popular from 1925 until the 1940's but was not named "Art Deco" until 1968 in a book by Bevis Hillier. During the 1930's, Tulsa was vying to be known as the "Oil Capital of the World" and was building opulent buildings to influence the rest of the world. Tulsa built an extraordinary number of Art Deco buildings for a city of its size. This book explores Tulsa's Art Deco through photographs to entertain you and encourage you to travel around Tulsa and experience the beauty of Art Deco.

Editors: Melissa Strakoulas and Mary Ellen Strakoulas

Acknowledgements:
My appreciation goes to Melissa Strakoulas and Mary Ellen Strakoulas for editing the book.

My thanks to Jennifer Wagner and Kent Sheely at Seed Technologies for the cover design and style recommendations.

Also thanks to Mike Wagner (WagTek Solutions) for our company website.

Dedication:
I dedicate this book to Mary Ellen Strakoulas, who is my constant source of encouragement and gets me though my difficult times. Thank you, my love.
Don Wagner

**Copyright 2009,
Oklahoma Tourist Guides Inc.,
All Rights Reserved**

All rights reserved under international and Pan-American copyright conventions. No part of this publication can be reproduced, stored in a retrieval system, or transmitted by any form, or by any means electronic, mechanical, photocopying recording or otherwise, without prior written permission of the copyright owner.

Published by:
Oklahoma Tourist Guides Inc.
3701 A South Harvard, #321
Tulsa, OK 74135

Printed in China

www.Tulsa-Books.com
Don.Wagner@Tulsa-Books.com

ISBN 978-1-4276-4201-1

Preface	1
Acknowledgements	1
Table of Contents	2
Art Deco Basics	3
Art Deco Styles	4
Book Organization	6
Art Deco Downtown	7
Union Depot	9
Boston Ave United Methodist Church	10
Warehouse / Farmers Market	16
Day & Nite Cleaners	19
Central High School	19
Service Pipeline	20
Fawcett Bldg.	20
OK Natural Gas	21
Public Service Co.	23
Gillete Tyrrell	24
Mayo Motor Inn	26
Tulsa Metro Bus Terminal	26
Day Building	27
South West Bell Dial Building	27
Philcade	28
Tulsa Club	32
Art Deco Mid-Town	33
Tulsa Fire Alarm Building	34
Adah Robinson Residence	36
Oak Lawn Cemetery Gate	37
Cities Service Station	37
Tulsa Monument Co	38
Milady's Cleaner	38
Guaranty Laundry	39
Hawks Dairies Company	39
J.B. Mc Gay Residence	40
William Whenthoff Residence	40
New Fire Station #7	41
National Guard Armory	41
Tulsa Fairgrounds Pavilion	42
New Fire Station #22	44
Stillwater Bank	44
Marquette School	45
Christ the King Parish	46
Shakespeare Monument	51
Art Deco South Tulsa	52
Ambassador Hotel	53
Phoenix Cleaners	54
Holland Hall School	54
Brook Theater	55
KVOO Studio	55
Baehler Brothers Service Station	56
City Veterinary	56
Arnold Ungerman Residence	57
Jesse Davis Residence	57
Westhope Richard Lloyd Jones Residence	58
Burtner Fleeger Residence	60
John D. Forsythe Residence	60
Home Federal Savings (BOK)	61
Howard J. Sherman Residence	62
Meyers Duren Harley	62
Art Deco North Tulsa	63
Fire Station #3	64
Mid West Marble & Tile	64
Oklahoma Department of Transportation	64
SW Bell Branch (Browns School)	64
Fire Station #16	65
Big Ten Ballroom	65
Animal Detention Center	66
New Fire Station #16	66
Fire Station #17	66
Fire Station #15	67
Will Rogers High School	67
Fire Station #7	70
Art Deco West Tulsa	71
Riverside Studio	72
Eleventh Street Arkansas River Bridge	74
Daniel Webster High School	75
Page Memorial Library	76
Central School Sand springs	76
Wheatley Brothers Foundry	77
Fire Station #13	77
Midwest Equitable Meter	77
Tulsa Designers of Art Deco	78
Gone but not Lost	79
You Decide - Retro Deco or Not	Back Cover

Art Deco Basics

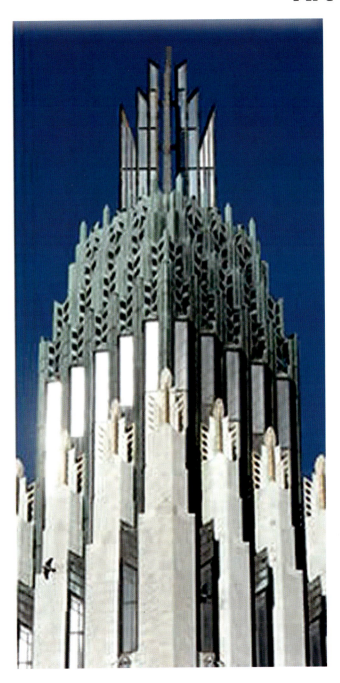

Introduction:
Art Deco evolved as a Modernist follow-up style to Art Nouveau during the 1930's. The austerity imposed by World War I resulted in a reaction to decorate buildings in a lavish and opulent style. In Scott Fitzgerald words, the distinctive style of Art Deco was "shaped by all the nervous energy stored up and unexpended in the War."

It was a new festive modern style that featured a variety of ornamentation and stylish motifs. Art Deco was less ostentatious and simpler than Art Nouveau, making it easier for mass production and construction. It was still an elegant design style dominant in decorative art. Where Art Nouveau focused on curves, Art Deco was centered on angles and geometric patterns.

It is important to remember that Art Deco is more than an Architectural style. It is also an art style that includes furniture, sculpture, clothing, jewelry and graphic designs.

The Art Deco style came from the 1925 Paris Exposition (Internationale des Arts Decoratifs Industriels et Modernes), that was held to celebrate modern world living. Even though the style was being defined, the actual term "Art Deco" wasn't coined until the late 1960s by art historian Bevis Hilliard. Before then the style was known as Zigzag modern, Jazz modern or Art Moderne. By 1940, the style had become unpopular and was being replaced by more progressive designs.

Art Deco is a culmination of exotic cultures, geometric shapes and the modern attitudes of a rapidly changing world of the 1930's and 1940's that resulted in a timeless style that still influences today's designs.

Tulsa History:
During Tulsa's Oil boom of the late 1920's, it became one of the important commerce cities in the country. Tulsan's had a great deal of money and a drive to prove to the rest of the world that they were a sophisticated and cosmopolitan city. Tulsa was trying to sell itself as the "Oil Capital" of the world. They pursued this by building skyscrapers and grand modern buildings beyond their necessity to impress the world.

The Art Deco style was the cutting edge architectural style that was both modern and decorative. As a result, Tulsa is one of the best Art Deco locations in the country and recognized world wide as a major Art Deco travel destination.

Art Deco Styles

The Art Deco style lacks a defining doctrine or manifesto so it fragmented into several different factions with unique attributes and features. It is an international architecture movement with significant influences from France, Cuba, Russia, Italy and the United States. In this country, there were three major styles of Art Deco. The earliest of the three was The Zigzag Styles that is vertically oriented and focused on angles and geometric designs. During the depression and through World War II, a shortage of materials and money resulted in the "Depression" or PWA (Publics Works Authority) version of Art Deco. Later the Streamline style, which was horizontally oriented and focused more on sleek curved structures became popular.

Zigzag

The Zigzag style was most popular through the 1920's and typically represents vertical buildings with geometric diagonal designs. The designs are sharp, angular and precise. Zigzag Art Deco designs are based on mathematical geometric shapes. These shapes are sometimes influenced by the art of ancient Egypt and Aztec Mexico.

The Zigzag style often decorates a building's façade with geometric ornamentation. It was an urban style that flourished in large cities like New York, Los Angeles and Miami. The Zigzag motif was primarily used for large commercial buildings; hotels, movie theaters, restaurants, department stores and skyscrapers. A luxurious assortment of materials; exotic wood veneers, marble, metals and painted terra-cotta were commonly used. These expensive and exotic materials were skillfully applied by period artisans.

PWA

The depression, caused by the stock market crash of 1931 launched President Franklin Roosevelt's New Deal to create construction jobs. The PWA (Public Works Authority) was one of the New Deal programs intended to build government and other public buildings. This resulted in a new style of Art Deco driven by the shortage of capital and materials. This style is referred to as the PWA or Depression Art Deco style. It has two separate manifestations in Tulsa. Many buildings were very scarce of funds and were produced with little artistic enhancements. Others, notably Will Rogers High School and Daniel Webster High School, were part of the Public Works Program where the government purposely financed the work of artisans, investing heavily in stone plaster and other construction art forms.

Streamline

The "Streamline" style was later phase of Art Deco that was heavily influenced by the shapes of modern transportation. Unlike previous versions of Art Deco, the streamline style was based on expectation and the future. It reflected the technological age that initiated air travel, telephone, radio, and talking pictures.

Its designs included aviation, electric lighting, radio and ocean liners. It also shows influences of jazz and the Hollywood film industry. Unlike the "Zigzag" style, the "Streamline" Art Deco was horizontal and featured aerodynamic curves and flowing forms. New materials; glass blocks, chrome, stainless steel, and neon signage are common to this style.

Modern

The Modern style, also referred to as "Art Moderne" came after the "Streamline" style and is characterized by asymmetrical cubic designs which often includes rounded corners. The Modern style is simple and unadorned with prolific art as were prior Art Deco styles. It is horizontally oriented with simple geometric shapes and little ornamentation and typically employs flat roofs. In Tulsa, many of fire stations employ this style.

Retro Deco

Many architects and designers are creating new building utilizing the Art Deco principles. These building are called retro deco, since they are retro fitting the old design principles into today's new building designs. This style utilizes features from the all the Art Deco styles and sometimes mixes features from the different styles. This gives new buildings a nostalgic appearance.

Book Organization

This book is organized to assist you in venturing through Tulsa to view the Art Deco sites described within these pages. The city is divided into sectors, so you may travel to each of the sites in the order in which they appear in the book. Each section is accompanied with an annotated map marking the art deco locations.

Art Deco Downtown

The Downtown District is defined as anywhere within Tulsa's downtown inter dispersal loop. Several of Tulsa's best Art Deco locations are within the downtown district and are best visited by car due to the distance between sites.

Downtown Art Deco Automobile Tour:

A - Union Depot (Page 9) Formerly Tulsa's train station.

B - Boston Avenue United Methodist Church (Page 10)
This is one of the country's best examples of Art Deco

C - Day & Nite Cleaner (Page 19)
On 11th Street, which coincides with Historic Route 66.

D - Warehouse/Farmers Market (Page 16) Colorful exterior and tower.

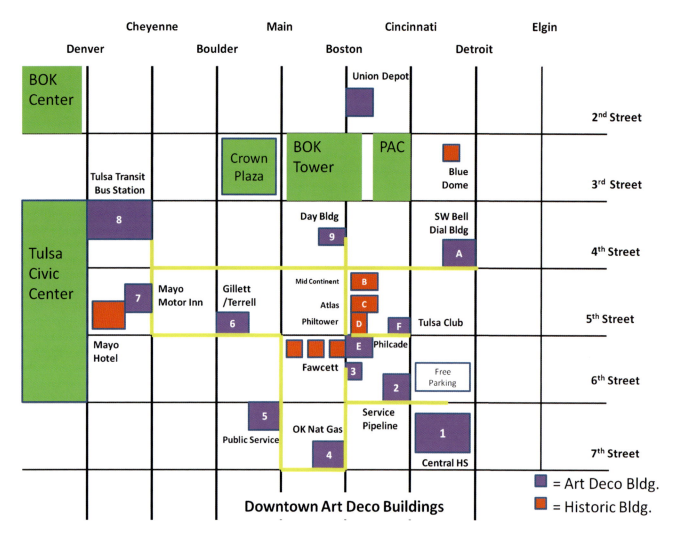

Downtown Art Deco Walking Tour:
1. **Central High School** — Page 19
2. **Service Pipeline** — Page 20
3. **Fawcett Building** — Page 20
4. **Oklahoma Natural Gas** — Page 21
5. **Public Service Company** — Page 23
6. **Gillett/Terrell Building** — Page 24
7. **Mayo Motor Inn** — Page 26
8. **MTTA Bus Station** — Page 26
9. **Day Building** — Page 27

A. **Southwest Bell Dial Building** - Art Deco on addition above 2nd   Page 28

B. **Philtower** — not Art Deco building, but each has a beautiful lobby
C. **Atlas Life Building** — that you will want to tour.
D. **Mid Continent Building** (Tulsa's most decorative lobby)

E. **Philcade** - The lobby is an art deco masterpiece   Page 29
F. **Tulsa Club**   Page 32

Tulsa Union Depot

Tulsa Union Depot served as Tulsa's train station for 38 years and totally ceased operation in 1967. The PWA style is expressed in its rugged utilitarian exterior. After deteriorating for a number of years, it was restored and recently has become the home of the Oklahoma Jazz Hall of Fame also known as Jazz Depot.

Built:	1931
Deco Style:	PWA
Designed By:	R. C. Stephens
NRIS:	84003458
Address:	3 S. Boston Ave.

Boston Avenue Methodist Church

"It's not a shame to look like other churches, but it's also wonderful to have one that doesn't look like any other church. That makes it special for people to come and see it," Dr. Mouzon Biggs of Boston Avenue Methodist Church.

Boston Avenue Methodist Church is an Art Deco masterpiece and landmark of significant national reputation. It is said to be the country's first church designed in a strictly American style of architecture.

Adah Robinson, an art teacher at Tulsa Central High School, was a member of the church and was asked by the ministry to assist in creating and selecting a design for a new church.

She studied the history and traditions of the church for a year prior to developing a design to incorporate the Methodist history and beliefs into the buildings design. She enlisted the assistance of her former student, Architect Bruce Goff, to transform her ideas into reality.

The church was designed by Goff to be viewed from all sides, not having a specific front or back. The exterior is decorated with numerous sculptures. The building utilizes metal, glass and terra cotta materials. For the exterior sculptures, Adah Robinson commissioned (another prior student) Robert Garrison.

The most prominent feature of the church is its 258 foot tower that houses 15 floors of useable office space.

On the south face of the church are the statues of the Circuit Riders, who were early Methodists spreading the word of God by horseback through Europe and America. The figures in the statue represent the first American Methodist bishop (Francis Asbury), Bishop William McKendrie and Rev. T.L. Darnell. Darnell was the father-in-law of the church minister and actually served as a circuit rider in America's early west.

Sixty Two pairs of praying hands are found in the ornamentation around the church's exterior. The hands are open in prayer signifying the openness to receive God's blessing.

"Closed lines and horizontal lines have been associated with finality. Modern lines are flowing, upward, open, and free. These modern hands, open are confident of the receptivity of Divine Grace."
                                              Adah Robinson

Built:	1929
Deco Style:	Zigzag
Architect:	Bruce Goff
	Rush, Endicott&Rush
Artist:	Adah Robinson
	Robert Garrison
Address:	
	1301 S. Boston Avenue

Over the north entrance of the building are statues of three founders of the Methodist religion (John Wesley, Charles Wesley and Susanna Wesley).

Seven pointed stars are used throughout the designs in the exterior and interior of the church. The seven points represent the seven heavenly virtues (patience, purity, knowledge, long suffering, kindness, love and truth).

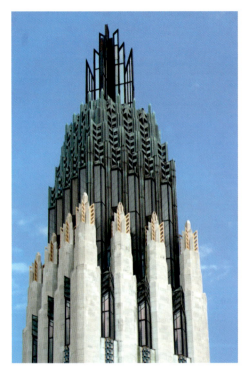

The terra cotta's golden color represents the light of God.

The dominant vertical lines represent the human spirit reaching upward to God.

The downward flowing lines represent the outpouring of Gods love.

The sanctuary is a semicircular design that uses the aisles and vertical lines to focus all to the pulpit. The design of the Moller pipe organ pipes and the doorway arches are angled arches representing a blessing on all in attendance.

Behind the pulpit is a huge mosaic (Author Johnson, 1960) with over 750,000 Venetian glass tiles. It duplicates the design of the stain glass windows and their downward flowing lines represent Gods outpouring of love. The art deco cross is indented symbolizing Christ once hung here but has risen.

   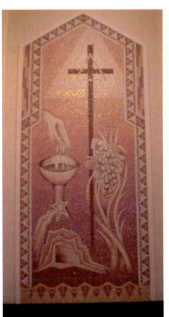

At either end of the Great Hall are large mosaics. The north wall depicts the burning bush and Torah representing the Old Testament. The south wall is representative of the New Testament.

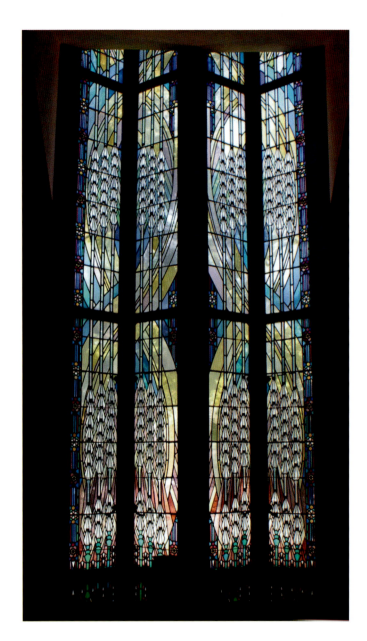 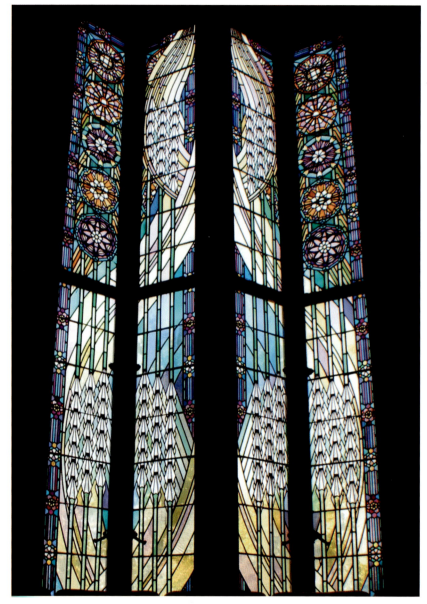

The interior art work of the church was designed by Adah Robinson. This included the beautiful stained glass windows. Unlike conventional churches you will not find humans portrayed in the designs. Adah Robinson grew up a Quaker and was influenced by their dictum against human representation in the sanctuary. The stain glass panels are not flat and are at a 45 degree angle to the exterior wall to assure access to light regardless of the sun's position. You will notice in the stained glass design the use of two Oklahoma indigenous flowers, the coreopsis and tritoma.

Warehouse/Farmers Market

The old Farmers market is a one-story building with a great terra cotta adorned tower. The "Farmers Market" was built in 1929 next to the railroad and served as a major grocery provider until the Great Depression.

It later became Club Lido and hosted famous musicians like Cab Calloway and Duke Ellington. In 1938, it was purchased by Warehouse Market and was a grocery store until 1978. It was used for several purposes after that but was poorly maintained and became severely run down.

Built: 1929
Deco Style: Zigzag
Designed By: B. Gaylord Noftsger
Address:
　　925 S. Elgin Avenue

Home Depot bought the property and had planned to demolish it and replace it with a new store. Local preservationists and the city of Tulsa negotiated with Home Depot to restore the building's frontage and build their store to the rear. Thankfully, this beautiful example of Art Deco was saved.

P.S. As a result of this restoration, Tulsans are very grateful to Home Depot and their store is very successful.

It has an entrance with two red medallions laying on blue backgrounds. One is representative of the progress of industry and displays a god holding an oil derrick and train engine. The other honors agriculture with a goddess holding a sheaf of wheat and a cornucopia.

Day & Nite Cleaner

Tulsa's Day & Nite Cleaners is a Route 66 vintage cleaner built in the streamline art deco style. It provides a distinct contrast to the zigzag styled Warehouse Market building across the street.

Its curved entrance and glass brick walls provide the sleek appearance common for the streamline style.

Built:	1946
Deco Style:	Streamline
Designed By:	William H. Wolaver
Address:	1012 South Elgin Avenue

Central High School

Central High School's 6th & Cincinnati building was originally built in 1916. At one time, it was the second largest high school in the country and included indoor Olympic-size lap pools, an indoor track, and an extensive art collection. Later, the school was moved from the downtown area. The original building was acquired by Public Service Company of Oklahoma and renovated for its headquarters.

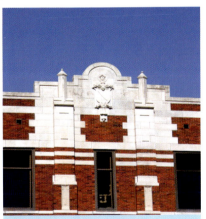

Built:	1929
Deco Style:	Zigzag
Designed By:	Coleman, Ervin & Associates
NRIS:	75001575
Address:	601 S. Cincinnati

Service Pipeline

Built: 1949
Deco Style: PWA
Designed By: Leon B. Senter
Address:
  520 S. Cincinnati Avenue

Fawcett Building

Built: 1934
Deco Style: Zigzag
Designed By: Leon B. Senter
Address:
  521 S. Boston Avenue

Oklahoma Natural Gas

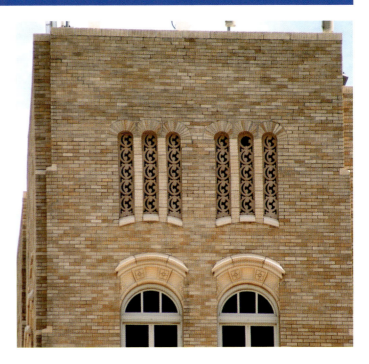

Tulsa had great financial growth in the late 1920's. This led Oklahoma Natural Gas to move its offices from Oklahoma City to Tulsa. Unusual for a conservative utility company, Oklahoma Natural chose to build a ten story Art Deco structure that set a benchmark for future Art Deco buildings in Tulsa. Notice the four piers on the face of the building that run vertical to the entire length of the building. Notice the telephone receivers inlaid in the tiles at the top of the building.

The interior design and materials are lavish. Oklahoma Natural Gas spent more than utility companies normally spent on public buildings to promote its success and impress the business people of Tulsa.

Built:	1928
Deco Style:	Zigzag
Designed By:	Arthur Atkinson
	Frederick Kershner
NRIS:	84003458
Address:	
	624 S. Boston Avenue

Public Service Company

The Public Service Company building was designed by the same company as the Oklahoma Natural Gas. It also was a conservative utility company trying to impress its customer base with an impressive Art Deco Building. The building features special exterior lighting designed to accentuate the fact that it was the electric company's building and visually present their expertise in lighting.

Built: 1929
Deco Style: Zigzag
Designed By: Arthur Atkinson
   Joseph Koberling
NRIS: 84003443
Address:
   600 S. Main Street

Gillette Tyrrell (Pythian)

The Gillette-Tyrell Building, often referred to as the Pythian, is one of Tulsa's significant Art Deco examples. Its appearance is unique both internally and externally. The building was originally designed to have thirteen floors but due to budget limitations was reduced to three. The exterior is covered by eye catching terracotta designs with vertical design and colorful Zigzag ornamentation.

Built: 1930
Deco Style: Zigzag
Designed By: Edward W. Saunders
NRIS: 82003703
Address: 423 S. Boulder

The lobby is richly decorated with colorful tile, mosaic floors, cast iron railings and etched glass light fixtures.

One of the attributes is a mezzanine that provides a great vista for all the decorated ornamentation on the walls and ceiling.

The designs include Italian, Spanish, and American Indian motifs.

Mayo Motor Inn

Built in 1950 for downtown automobile parking the Mayo Motor Inn features ribbon windows and a fifteen foot green sign crowned with three white bars.

Built: 1950
Deco Style: Streamline
Designed By: Leon B. Senter & Associates
Address:
　　416 S. Cheyenne Avenue

Tulsa Metro Bus Terminal

The Downtown Metro Bus Terminal was built to consolidate the location for transfer between buses to a single downtown site. This also relieved congestion caused by multiple bus stops on the downtown streets. The Art Deco Style of the building and departure bays provide a visual treat for travelers. Be sure to notice the murals over the ticket counters inside the terminal.

Built: 1999
Deco Style: Retro
Designed By: HTB, Inc
Address:
　　3rd & Cheyenne Avenue

Day Building

The Day Building was the home to a Tulsa landmark (Nelson's Buffeteria). Nelson's opened in 1929 and was known around the country for its chicken fried steak   Currently the building is used by the eco-friendly Elot's café.

Built: 1926
Deco Style: Zigzag
Designed By: Bruce Goff
Address:
512 S. Boston Avenue

Southwestern Bell Main Dial Building

The first two floors of the building were constructed in 1924 in the Gothic Style. The purpose of the building was to house the switching boards and operators required to make telephone connections.

Six years later they expanded the building an additional four floors utilizing the Zigzag Art Deco style. A vertical pair of terra cotta shields is located above the torches. Above the second floor the building facade has Stepped back panels that run from the second floor to the roof line. At that point terra cotta ornamentation completes the building's pinnacles.

Built: 1924
Deco Style: Zigzag
Designed By: I.R. Timlin
NRIS: 84003445
Address:
424 South Detroit Avenue

Philcade

Built: 1930
Deco Style: Zigzag
Designed By: Smith & Senter
NRIS: 86002196
Address:
 511 S. Boston

Waite Philips built the Philcade Building in part to protect his business investment in the Philtower, located just north of the Philcade. At that time the principle Tulsa merchant area was on Main Street between 4th and 5th Street. Several merchants were planning to move their stores to locations on South Boulder which would have diverted Tulsa's of growth away from the Philtower, thus decreasing its value.

To abate this prospect, Waite Phillips planned to build the nine story Philcade with the lower two stories housing an Arcade of 28 retail shops. The upper floors were office space for the expanding Tulsa Oil industry. The buildings structure was overbuilt to allow the 1930's addition of four more floors.

The ground-level highlights store showcase windows and very decorative entrances. The building entrances are flanked by Egyptian styled columns terminated by terra cotta beams.

From the third floor to the roofline is a combination of exterior veneer, patterned brick and large steel double hung windows The terra cotta heavily utilizes a stylized flora and fauna.

There is an eighty foot brick tunnel between the Philtower and Philcade that caused considerable construction problems but functionally connects the two buildings.

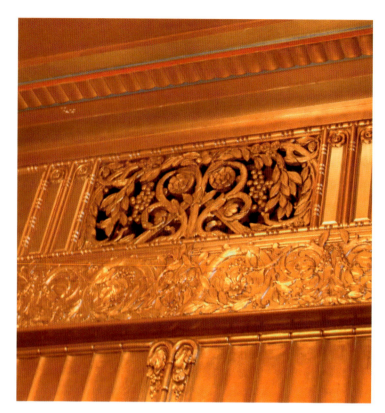

The art work in the lobby of the Philcade is quite significant. The decorations are lavish with fluted and polished marble, ornamental plaster covered with gold leaf over tan and black terrazzo floors. The ceiling is covered with gold leaf and hand painted with geometric designs displayed in the Zigzag Art Deco style. The retail store units have mahogany, glass, and bronze detailed store fronts.

Tulsa Club

Construction of the Tulsa Club was a collaboration between the Tulsa Chamber of Commerce and the Tulsa Club. Floors one through five were occupied by the Chamber while the top six floors and the roof garden were the domain of the Tulsa Club.

The Tulsa Club, organized in 1923, was the most prestigious social and athletic club in Tulsa. The wealthiest Tulsans including Waite Phillips were members and used its facilities. They had dormitory rooms, a men's lounge, a gymnasium, a barber shop and gardens on the roof.

The distinctive black tiles were added some time after the original construction are not scene in earlier pictures. The building is currently abandoned and in disrepair.

Built: 1927
Deco Style: Zigzag
Designed By: Bruce Goff
Address: 115 East 5th St.

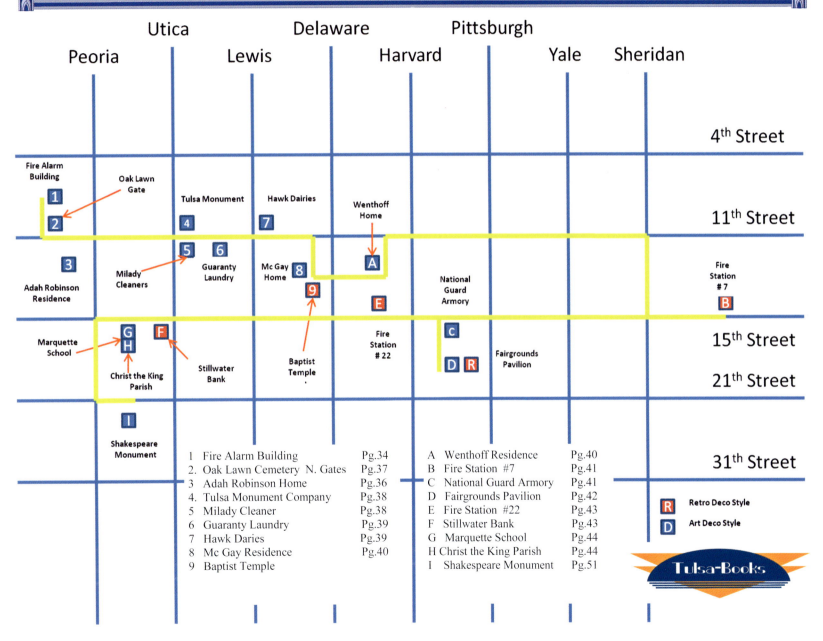

Tulsa Fire Alarm Building

The Fire Alarm (1934) building was built to centralize the fire alarm systems for all of Tulsa. They would dispatch firemen from various parts of the city as needed. This octagonal building features terra cotta frieze work depicting a Mayan culture theme with double headed dragons connected to stylized hoses with the nozzles.

The exterior of the building has considerable terra cotta decoration. The Mayan Temple design was influenced by an award-winning design that Frederick Kershner, the building's architect, had earlier won from the Beaux Arts Institute of New York City.

Built:	1930
Deco Style:	PWA
Designed By:	Frederick V. Kershner
NRIS:	03000879
Address:	1010 E. 8th Street

The terra cotta panel above the front door features a male figure with alarm communications tape running through his hands. To either side are helmeted firefighters. Below him are two dragons with fire hoses making up their head. The front façade uses a recurring theme of a double-headed dragon which are common in Mayan culture and refer to gathering of energy from the earth. At the rear of the building are four gargoyle-like sculptures topped with a hatchet.

Adah Robinson Residence

Adah Robinson was a significant figure in the development of Art Deco in Tulsa. She is principle designer of the Boston Avenue Methodist Church. While designing the church, she used her earnings to build her home. Two of her prior students and prominent architects, Bruce Goff and Joseph Koberling Jr. (Biographies ... page 80) assisted her. Adah, not being a domestically inclined, failed to design an adequate kitchen for the house. Her friend, Mrs. Mc Arthur, pointed out the flaw and the need for a real kitchen. Adah and Joseph Koberling spent the entire evening redesigning the house to fit in a kitchen. Features of the house include Art deco styled windows, light fixtures, a sunken fireplace and built-in angular furniture.

Built:	1927 & 1929
Deco Style:	Zigzag
Designed By:	Bruce Goff
	Joseph Koberling
Artist:	Adah Robinson
Address:	1119 S. Owasso

Oak Lawn Cemetery Gate

Across the street from Tracy Park are the Art Deco Gates to Oak Lawn Cemetery.

Built: 1930
Deco Style: PWA
Designed By: Unknown
Address: 11th & Peoria Ave.

Cities Service Station

This is a typical example of the streamline design that was adopted for many gasoline filling stations across the country in the 1930's.

The idea was to make them look sleek, easily identifiable as a gas station and branded by appearance to the petroleum manufacture.

Built: 1930
Deco Style: Streamline
Designed By: M.R. Pettingill
Address:
    1303 East 11th Street

Tulsa Monument Company

The 1936 Tulsa Monument building is an Art Deco structure designed to simulate the appearance of a burial monument. The most prominent feature is the clock tower at its entrance.

The white concrete building has gray trim that draws attention to the roof-line and windows. It utilizes the three bands as caps to the vertical elements of the building. This is a fine example of the "3-Bar Modern" architectural design style.

Built:	1936
Deco Style:	Streamline
Designed By:	Harry H. Mahler
NRIS:	08000849
Address	1535 E. 11th St.

Milady's Cleaner

The lower half of this two story building is covered with an undecorated light terra cotta that simulates cut stone blocks. There is a sharp contrast between these light cream colored blocks and the black marble appearance surrounding the doors and display windows.

Built:	1930
Deco Style:	Zigzag
Designed By:	Unknown
Address:	1736 E. 11th St.

Guaranty Laundry

The building features horizontal bands above and below windows that surround the structure.

In 1940, Koberling & Fleming added a fur storage unit to the building.

Built: 1928, 1940
Deco Style: Zigzag
Designed By: Bruce Goff (1928)
Koberling & Fleming (1940)
Address: 2036 East 11th Street

Hawks Dairies Company

As an example of post-World War II Modernist architecture, Hawk Dairies was a processor for over 600 local dairy farmers. Its products were distributed over a six state region.

A huge ice cream parlor once serviced the public on the first floor of the building.

Built: 1948
Deco Style: PWA
Designed By: Gerad W. Wolf
Jack Owen Stegall
NRIS: 08000854
Address: 2415 E. 11th St.

J.B. McGay Residence

JJ. B. McGay was one of Tulsa's most successful inventors having designed the tube-less tire, parking meter and the gas calculator used at filling stations.

His five level home is of the Streamline Art Deco style with some Zigzag elements included. It incorporated many new features for its time like corner windows and a garage at the front of the house. McGay worked 4 years with Joseph Koberling on the design of the house.

Built: 1936
Deco Style: Streamline
Designed By: Joseph R. Koberling, Jr.
Address: 1551 South Yorktown Pl.

William Whenthoff Residence

The front of the William D. Whenthoff house resembles an ocean liner's bridge with its deck railing and port hole.

This two-story stream-lined ship style uses tile blocks painted to look like stucco.

Built: 1935
Deco Style: Streamline
Designed By: Unknown
Address: 1142 South College Ave.

New Fire Station #7

This is a new station that replaced the old Fire Station #7 at 6th & Lewis (see page 71). This building is constructed in your Retro Art Deco style.

Built:
Deco Style: Retro
Designed By:
Address: 15th St. & 74th E. Avenue

National Guard Armory

The National Guard Armory is a good example of the austere PWA architecture.

It has very few exterior adornments, which is a sharp contrast to the PWA style represented by the Fair Grounds Pavilion located just down the street.

This building was once the home site for Tulsa University basketball games.

Built: 1942
Deco Style: PWA
Designed By: A.M. Atkinson
Address: 3902 E. 15th Street

Tulsa Fairgrounds Pavilion

Built in 1932, the Fair Grounds Pavilion is a PWA style building. The gold brick building features very attractive terra cotta ornamentation. Each of its eight entrances has decorative terra cotta depicting horse, cattle and ram heads.

It is unusual for a building built in this time period to be so ornamental. It is representative of government financed programs to support out of work craftsmen and artists during the depression.

Built: 1932
Deco Style: PWA
Designed By: Leland I. Shumway
Address:
    Expo Square 21st & Jamestown

Central Park Hall Building

Built: 2008
Deco Style: Retro
Designed By: Unknown
Address: Expo Square 21st & Yale

New Fire Station #22

This is another replacement fire station that utilizes the Retro Art Deco Style.

Built:
Deco Style: Retro
Designed By: Unknown
Address: 15th St. & College Avenue

Stillwater Bank

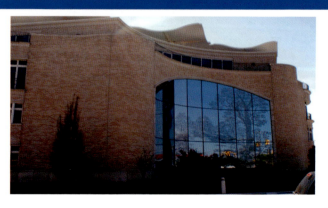

This Retro Art Deco Style building is reminiscent of the Moderne Style with it's curved sides and artistic flair.

The huge etched glass windows are especially stunning when lit at night.

Built:
Deco Style: Retro
Designed By: Unknown
Address: 15th St. & Utica Avenue

Marquette School

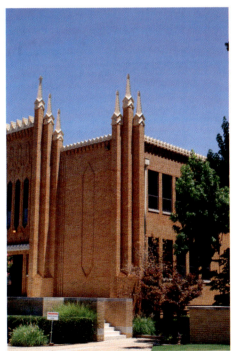

Marquette is a Catholic School and part of Christ the King Parish. It was styled to coordinate with Christ The King Parish, an adjacent building to its south.

Built: 1932
Deco Style: Zigzag
Designed By: Federick W. Redlich
Address: 1519 S. Quincy Ave.

Christ the King Parish

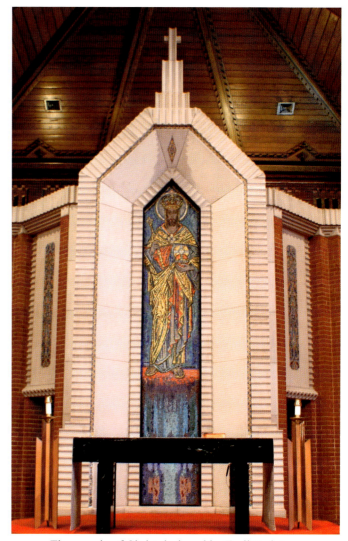

The mosaic of Christ designed by Emil Frei, Inc.

Bishop Francis Kelly, for whom Bishop Kelly High School is named, brought Francis Byrne from Chicago to design a church that was "something both modern and authentic to Catholic worship". Byrne, who had worked for Frank Lloyd Wright in Chicago, utilized a Zigzag design incorporating Gothic and Byzantine features. The design was so innovative and radical that many local Catholics were outraged by it.

Built:	1929
Deco Style:	Zigzag
Designed By:	Francis Barry Byrne
	Bruce Goff
Artist:	Alphonso Iannelli
Address:	16th S Quincy Ave.

Alfonso Iannelli was hired to be the primary art designer and was responsible for the terra-cotta ornamentation including the spires around the exterior of the building and design of the stained glass windows.

The design of the sanctuary is essentially square with strong vertical influences. The sanctuary is crowned by a ceiling of dark polished wood slats. The two mosaics over the side alters were designed by Tulsa architect Bruce Goff.

When the church was dedicated in 1928, it was the first church in the world to be dedicated as "Christ the King".

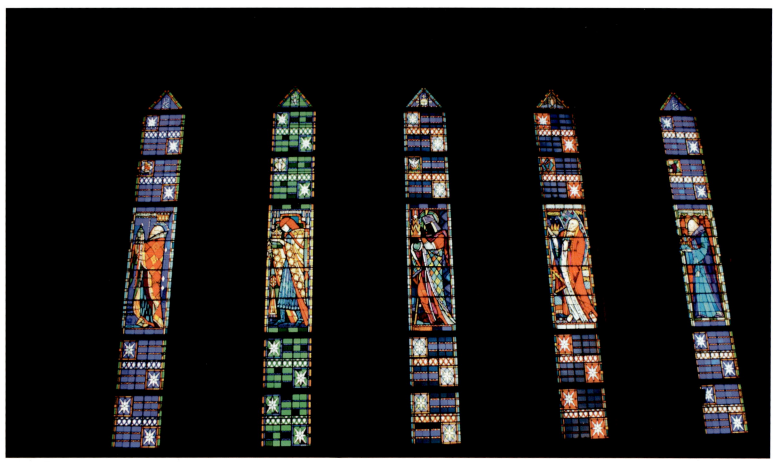
Italian Artist Alphonso Iannelli designed the stain glass windows and interior art work. The windows were produced by the Temple Art Glass Company of Chicago . The windows depict five Saints and five Kings of the Christian era. The kings are all carrying their crowns in respect to Christ who is wearing his crown in the mosaic over the alter.

Shakespeare Monument

Woodward Park has an Art Deco style monument to English playwright William Shakespeare.

The design was done by Adah Robinson with assistance from sculptor Eugene Shonnard.

Built: 1932
Deco Style: Zigzag
Designed By: Adah Robinson
　　　　　　　Eugene Shonnard
Address:
　　Woodward Park

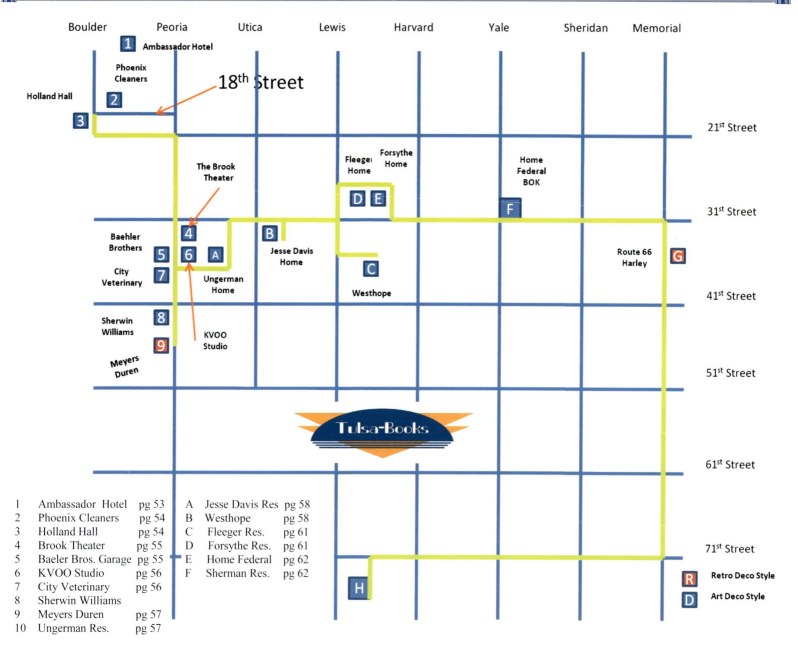

Ambassador Hotel

The Ambassador Hotel is a ten-story Mediterranean style building with Zigzag Art Deco feature. It is a beautiful structure, graced with Italian terra cotta relief panels and limestone cornices. Notice how the vertical nature of the building is accentuated by the decorative stonework.

It was built in 1929 to provide upscale temporary housing for oil barons and their families while they built their mansions. It was one of the countries first "extended stay" hotels. The Ambassador is also the location of The Chalkboard, one of Tulsa's finest restaurants.

Built:	1929
Deco Style:	Zigzag
Designed By:	N.E. Peters & Smith & Senter
Address:	1324 S. Main Street

Phoenix Cleaners

Phoenix Cleaners is a two-story, brick building built in the Art Deco Streamline Moderne style.

It uses glass bricks, smooth lines and a curved front corner.

The front façade has black metal window canopies and a green and white neon signs.

Built: 1947
Deco Style: Streamline
Designed By: Singletary
Address: 125 E. 18th Street

Holland Hall School (Boulder on the Park)

Wealthy Tulsan's Waite Phillips, W.G. Skelly and George S. Bole person-ally financed the building of Holland Hall School. The school moved in 1938 to a location around 28th and College. In 1947, the building was acquired by KTUL Radio who remodeled the building in the Art Deco Stream-line Style. The building served as their broadcast studio. It was adorned with a neon KTUL sign. They referred to the building on the radio as "Boulder on the Park". They quit broadcasting from that location in 1955.

Built: 1923
Deco Style: Streamline
Designed By: Charles A. & Roy W. Sanderson
NRIS: 03000872
Address: 1850 South Boulder Ave.

Brook Theater

Originally the Brook Theater and now the Brook Restaurant and Bar was built in 1945 in the Streamline Art Deco style. The six hundred seat theater was famous for its "Saturday afternoon matinees". Tulsa book lovers remember the Lewis Meyer Book Store adjacent to the theater.

Both these areas have been incorporated into the Brook Restaurant and Bar. The Bar retains much of the Art Deco Appearance including an art styled entrance and streamline curvatures to the building expansions.

Built:	1945
Deco Style:	Streamline
Designed By:	William Henry Cameron Calderwood
Address:	3401 S. Peoria Avenue

KVOO Studio

The Brookside Broadcast Center (now KJRH-TV) is a streamline style of art deco featuring a very large tower streaking into the sky.

Built:	1956
Deco Style:	Streamline
Designed By:	Koberling Brandenbourg
Address:	3701 S. Peoria Ave.

Baehler Brothers Service Station

Now a studio this building still retains its sleek art deco streamline features.

Built: 1950
Deco Style: Streamline
Designed By: Frederick V. Kershner
Address: 3702 S. Peoria Avenue

City Veterinary

The City Veterinary Hospital is a Streamline styled Art Deco building with a flat roof, rounded corners and large curved glass block windows.

The buff colored brick structure has a banded parapet and horizontal inlaid brick stripes that compliment its sleek streamlined features.

In 1942, this building was built as a veterinary clinic. It retains its original purpose, despite attempts by real-estate developers to acquire the property.

Built: 1942
Deco Style: Streamline
Designed By: Joseph R. Koberling
NRIS: 08000848
Address: 3550 S. Peoria Avenue

Sherwin Williams

Built:
Deco Style: Retro
Designed By:
Artist:
Address: 47th & Peoria Ave.

Meyers Duren Harley

This retro deco facility sports features from the streamline art deco style. The pastel salmon and turquoise stripes accentuate its sleek style.

This building portrays a passenger ship imagery. Notice the circular portal windows along the sides. From the front it resembles an ocean liner bridge.

Built:
Deco Style: Retro
Designed By:
Artist:
Address: 47th & Peoria Ave.

Arnold Ungerman Residence

This house was intended to be a combination Mexican-Southwestern and contemporary modern styles. It turned out to be a Streamline style two story, art-deco house with horizontal bands at the roof line. It has a concrete block structure on top of a slab foundation that features corner windows, and a glass-block curved bay.

Built: 1941
Deco Style: Streamline
Designed By: Leo Clark
Address: 1718 East 37th Street

Jesse Davis Residence

This concrete Streamline Art Deco house is designed to portray the image of a ship. The interior features a three story spiral staircase surrounding a two foot column.

Francis Davis, a student of Adah Robinson designed Tulsa's first all Electric Home. In 1937, they held a public open house hosting five thousand visitors in seven hours.

Built: 1936
Deco Style: Streamline
Designed By: Frances Davis
Address: 3231 S. Utica Avenue

Westhope (Richard Lloyd Jones Residence)

Westhope, the residence of Richard Lloyd Jones, was built by his cousin Frank Lloyd Wright. Jones, a wealthy man, was owner of "The Tribune" one of Tulsa's two major newspapers.

The original designs were for a Japanese style house of wood and stucco. Wright changed his mind upon visiting the site for the house. The new design was a block design with concrete vertical pillars. The concrete blocks were actually molded on the construction site.

Westhope is very spatial and reminds one more of a museum than a home. Notice the vertically stacked windows between the columns that produce what Wright calls a transparent screen.

Each Frank Lloyd Wright house incorporates carved exterior blocks with unique decorative design that are duplicated nowhere else. The block pattern on the left, serves as a distinct trademark for Westhope. This Mayan pattern is used through the interior and exterior of the house.

Built: 1929
Deco Style: Zigzag
Designed By: Frank Lloyd Wright
NRIS: 75001575
Address:
    3704 S. Birmingham Avenue

Westhope is extraordinarily modern considering it was built in 1929. It is very spatial and had a chilled water system for cooling. Other features included an open floor plan that traverses over multiple plateaus. The flat roof of tar covered by pitch stones was a new building innovation of Wright's that he introduced with this home. This two story 10,000 square foot house had a four car garage, garden room, pool, fish pond, formal garden areas, and four patios.

Burtner Fleeger Residence

This Streamline style residence is built on an uneven lot, resulting in stair stepped roof levels and balconies. It was Tulsa's first solid concrete home fulfilling the owners wishes for an easy to clean exterior.

Its exterior features striated narrow horizontal bands and a glass block wall on the side of the house. The front location of the garage was unique for the 1930's.

Built: 1937
Deco Style: Streamline
Designed By: Frederick V. Kershner
Address: 2424 E. 29th Street

John D. Forsythe Residence

This two-story, flat roofed house was designed as a gift to Johns wife Anne who wanted a home modern for the time. It has a low concrete landscaping wall across the front of the property that extends the original house design. It portrays the appearance of a ship with strong horizontal features.

Forsythe was a prominent local architect having designed the Southern Hills Country Club Clubhouse, All Souls Unitarian Church and Daniel Webster High School.

Built: 1937
Deco Style: Streamline
Designed By: John Duncan Forsyth
Address: 2837 S. Birmingham Pl.

Home Federal Savings (BOK)

Built: 1956
Deco Style: Streamline
Designed By: Koberling & Brandborg
Address: 31st & Harvard

Howard J. Sherman Residence

Mr. Sherman was an early employee of Philips petroleum and used his profits from that business venture to move to Tulsa and become an oil investor.

His residence was often referred to as "The Farm" because he raised turkeys in grounds surrounding the house.

Built: 1937
Deco Style: Streamline
Designed By: E.H. Mattern Co.
Address: 7228 S. Evanston Ave.

North Tulsa Art Deco

1	Fire Station #3	pg.64
2	Midwest Marble	pg.64
3	OK Dept of Trans.	pg.64
4	SW Bell Branch	pg.64
5	Fire Station #16	pg.65
6	Big Ten Ballroom	pg.65
7	Animal Detention SPCA	pg.66
8	New Fire Station #16	pg.66
9	Fire Station #17	pg.66
A	Fire Station #15	pg.67
B	Will Rogers High School	pg.67
C	Old Fire Station #7	pg.70

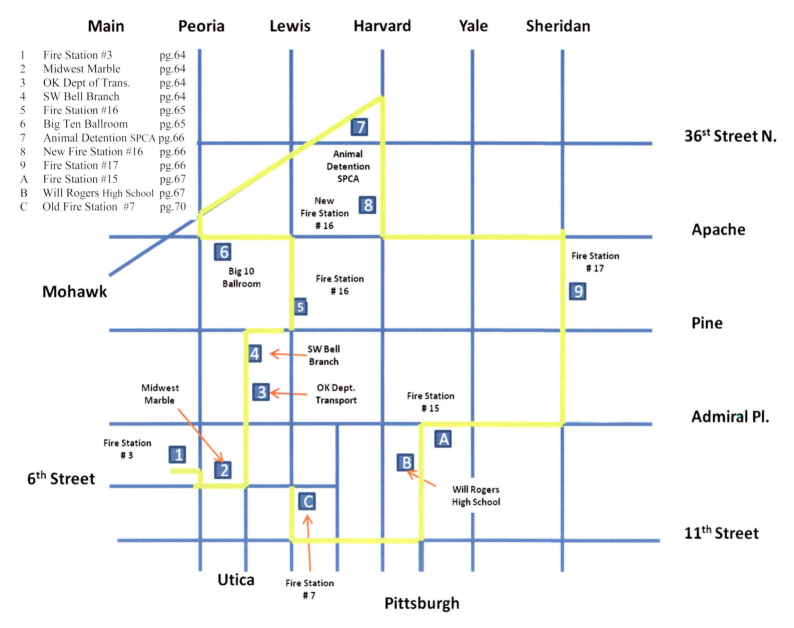

Old Fire Station #3

The Old Fire Station #3 features metallic deco styled ledges over the doors and windows.

The station services and designation were moved to 1339 E. 1st in 1948.

Built: 1909
Deco Style: Modern
Designed By: Merry Screen Co.
Advantage Glass
Address: 1013 E. 3rd. St.

Midwest Marble

Midwest Marble Company cut, polished and installed marble in Tulsa buildings and homes. Its building reflected their craftsmanship utilizing black and white marble tiles along its front face. Its two horizontal stripes below the roofline give it a very streamlined appearance. Also unique is how the walls curve inward at the entrance

Built: 1945
Deco Style: Streamline
Designed By: Robert E. West
Address: 507 South Quaker Ave.

OK Dept. of Transportation

Originally the Tulsa headquarters of the Oklahoma Department of Transportation, this relatively square building features an art-deco styled stonework at its entrance.

Built: 1940
Deco Style: PWA
Designed By: E.W. Saunders
Ivan Richardson
Address: 1709 E. King Place

SW Bell Branch

The building, built as a Southwestern Bell branch office, features streamline features with curved corners. It recently has been used as a substance abuse center.

Built:
Deco Style: Streamline
Designed By:
Artist:
Address: 1333 N. Utica Ave.

Old Fire Station #16

Fire Station #16 was one of Tulsa's oldest active stations. In 2009, a new Station #16 was built near Apache and Harvard (see page 67). The new station utilizes a Retro Deco style of architecture.

Built:	1947
Deco Style:	Modern
Designed By:	John W. Robb
Address:	1401 N. Lewis Ave

Big Ten Ballroom

Lonny Williams, one of Tulsa's first black police officers, had the Big Ten Ballroom built in 1948 to provide a performance venue for black entertainers. It is a large open structure with streamline curved corners with railings along the roof.

Built:	1948
Deco Style:	Streamline
Designed By:	Unknown
Address:	1632 E. Apache Ave

Animal Detention Center

The old animal detention center currently houses the Tulsa Society for the Prevention of Animals (SPCA),

It is a typical example of the PWA art deco style designed with classic lines and very little exterior adornment.

Built: 1931
Deco Style: PWA
Designed By: Rush, Endacott & Rush
Address: 2910 Mohawk Blvd.

New Fire Station #16

The new Fire Station 16 replaced the station at 1401 N. Lewis (See page 66) and is built in the Retro Deco style.

It is Tulsa's first fire station designed with individual sleeping quarters for firefighters, thus providing reasonable accommodations for Tulsa's women firefighters.

Built:
Deco Style: Retro
Designed By:
Address: 2302 N. Harvard

Fire Station #17

Fire Station #17 is a typical modern style art deco building with an asymmetrical cubic design with a horizontal orientation and little exterior ornamentation.

Built: 1947
Deco Style: Modern
Designed By: Hanton & Wilson
Address: 1351 N. Sheridan

Fire Station #15

Fire Station #15 is a modern style art deco building.

Notice how the roofline and pillars highlight the cubic nature of the design. The covered porch accentuates the horizontal design.

Built:	1947
Deco Style:	Modern
Designed By:	
Address:	4162 E. Admiral

Tulsa Will Rogers High School

Architect Joseph Koberling's On Will Rogers High School

"We felt that it should be a worthy tribute and memorial to a man every one loved so well. It seemed to us, that the building should be monumental in character. However, because it was a school, it should not be a somber type of a monumental memorial. Rather it should be alive and joyous in character, not only reflecting his own outlook on life, but also the spirit and aspirations of the generations of young men and women who were to use this structure as a place of learning and training to become useful citizens throughout the coming years.

The vertical lines, the massing of the entrances, the ornamentation, and the selection of materials and colors throughout the project were deliberately studied to produce this desired effect. "

Will Rogers High School

Will Rogers High School is a PWA period Art Deco building with extraordinary embellishments for its time. Typical PWA style buildings were very lacking in ornate fixtures and relied on structural features to make the Art Deco impression. The front of the building features two towers supported by stepped pilasters topped with ornate terra cotta capitals.

Above the double doors are panels that depict the cowboy and movie periods of Will Rogers' life.

Built: 1938
Deco Style: PWA
Designed By: Leon B. Senter
Joseph R. Koberling
NRIS: 07000918
Address: 3909 E. 5th Place

The interior of the building is spectacular with its terrazzo floors, tile walls and ornate gold leaf decorated doorways and enclaves. The auditorium is an art deco treat from the chairs to the deco lights above.

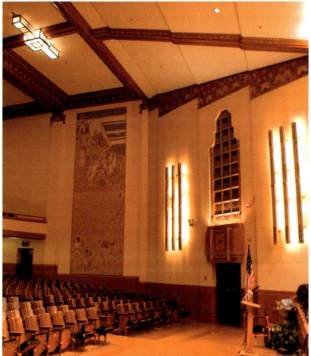

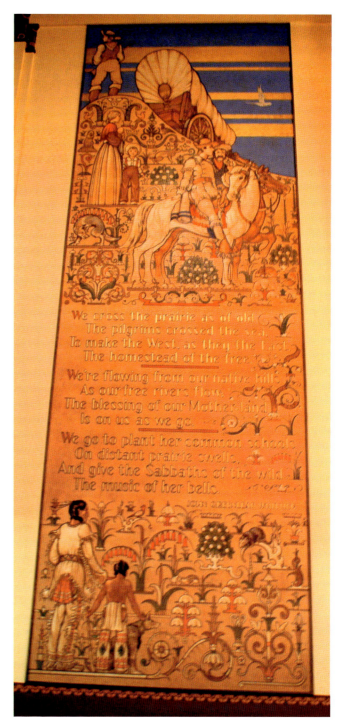

Old Fire Station #7

Fire Station #7 was one of Tulsa's earliest Fire Stations. A new Station #7, of Retro Art Deco influence was built at 3005 E. 15th Street, .(see Page 41). The old building is occupied by a landscaping company. The original glass block panels are still visible on the east building face.

Built: 1921
Deco Style: Modern
Re Modeled: 1948, 1967
Design By: Joseph Koberling
Address: 601 S. Lewis Ave.

Art Deco West Sector

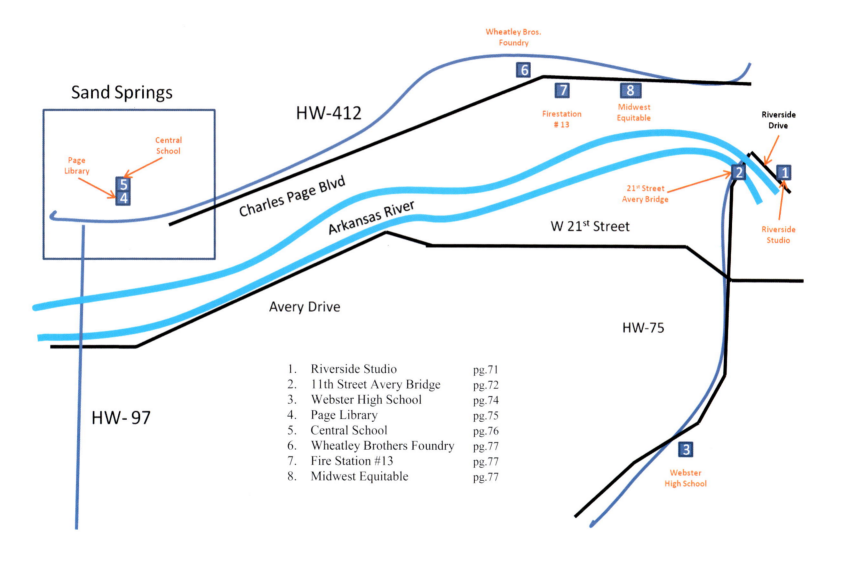

1. Riverside Studio — pg.71
2. 11th Street Avery Bridge — pg.72
3. Webster High School — pg.74
4. Page Library — pg.75
5. Central School — pg.76
6. Wheatley Brothers Foundry — pg.77
7. Fire Station #13 — pg.77
8. Midwest Equitable — pg.77

Riverside Studio

Only 2 blocks south of the Avery memorial is an Art Deco treasure. The Riverside Studio currently houses a theater that puts on weekly production of "The Drunkard" a "The Drunkard" /olio with audience participation. Be sure and check out the stunning art deco murals on the walls. Performances of the "The Drunkard and Olio" can be attended Saturday evenings 7:45 p.m. curtain call.
(Reservations 918-587-5030)

The Riverside Studio was designed by Bruce Goff as a combination music studio, performance venue and residence for Patty Shriner. Mrs. Shriner had eight music studios in Tulsa providing music lessons. She wanted a studio to hold large recital performances and offer music lessons.

The design of the building reflects the music theme. The square exterior windows replicate the holes in player piano tape. The slats in the round window were designed to abstractly resemble keys on a piano keyboard.

Olinka Hrdy was hired by Goff to paint 9 abstract pictures for the interior of the studio.

Mrs. Shriner disliked the color schemes and argued endlessly with Bruce Goff and Olinka Hrdy about the paintings and colors Hrdy once told Shriner "There is only one color you should use." When Shriner asked "What color is that?" She replied "White! White is the color of insanity".

Olinka Hrdy got the last word on the issue. Shriner disliked jazz and insisted there be no reference to it in the artwork or designs.

Hrdy's paintings imbedded the word "JAZZ" within the abstract design so it was only visible when photographed in black and white.

Built:	1929
Deco Style:	Zigzag
Designed By:	Bruce Goff
Artist:	Olinka Hrdy
NRIS:	01000656
Address:	1381 S. Riverside Dr.

Cyrus Avery / 11th Street Bridge

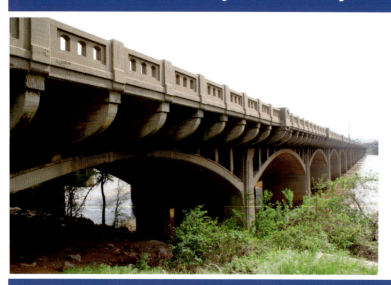

The 11th Street Bridge is a good example of a multi-span concrete arch bridge with verticals creating a continuous span constructed of reinforced concrete. The roadway decking and guardrails are monolithic. It was altered in 1929 and has ornate guardrails utilizing Art Deco zigzag motifs.

This Art Deco bridge has significant historical relevance. When Route 66 was being organized into the first national highway the it was the only highway bridge over the Arkansas River. As a result Route 66 was diverted south through Tulsa.

Built:	1917
Deco Style:	PWA
Designed By:	
NRIS:	96001488
Address:	11th & Riverside Dr

Webster High School

Daniel Webster High School

Daniel Webster High School opened in 1938 and was built using Works Progress Administration (WPA) funds. Out of work artisans were employed to create a buff brick Art Deco structure. It has a very impressive entrance flanked with large rectangular columns. Two large metal torch lanterns flank the front entrance with the school name and a large clock hanging above. The aluminum plaques above the doors are of a classic Greek motif.

Built: 1938
Deco Style: PWA
Designed By: Arthur Atkinson
　　　　　　　John Duncan Forsyth
　　　　　　　Raymond Kerr
　　　　　　　William H. Wolaver
NRIS: 01000656
Address: 1919 W. 40th

Page Memorial Library

Built: 1929
Deco Style: Zigzag
Designed By: Otis Floyd Johnson
Address:
6 E. Broadway, Sand Springs

Central School

Built: 1950
Deco Style: Streamline
Designed By: Joseph Kobering
Address:
Broadway, Sand Springs

Wheatley Brothers Foundry

Wheatley Bros Foundry & Machine Co. is a 1940's building with strong Zigzag art deco features. The building is currently being used by Tulsa Housing Authority.

Built: 1940's
Deco Style: Zigzag
Designed By: Joseph Kobering
Address: 33rd West Avenue & Charles Page Blvd

Fire Station #13

The station displays strong zigzag art deco influences. It was later replaced by a new Fire Station #13 at 345 S. 41st W. Ave.

Built: 1933
Deco Style: Zigzag
Designed By: Unknown
Address: 3924 Charles Page Blvd

Midwest Equitable Meter

The Midwest Equitable Meter Building is a tan brick commercial warehouse that was designed by Bruce Goff. It features glass blocks along the side of the building.

Tulsa-Books
www.Tulsa-Books.Com
(918) 693-1198

Built: 1929
Deco Style: Zigzag
Designed By: Bruce Goff
Address: 3130 Charles Page Blvd

Tulsa Designers of Art Deco

Adah Robinson (1882-1962)

Adah was a remarkable woman who came to Tulsa after serving as a Professor of Art at the University of Oklahoma. She took a position teaching at Tulsa High School (later renamed Central) and developed one of the top high school art programs in the nation. She had a passion for art that had profound influence on others. She developed what amounted to a city planning program for her students. They surveyed Tulsa's downtown block by block to determine the relationship of building styles to the needs and the relationship between building styles. Bruce Goff and Joe Koberling were students that became prominent art deco architects.

Adah was an extraordinary organizer and supporter of the arts. She created "Chaioscuro" club to promote social activities and the love of fine art. It hosted several million dollar art exhibits at the high school that brought in old master collections from New York, Pennsylvania and Kansas City. She gathered a significant collection of art for school and even came up with a "penny a week" donation campaign to raise money to purchase art work for the schools corridors.

She was a member and Director of Art for Boston Avenue Methodist church when they were looking to build a new church at 13th & Boston. She created the design and presented sketches of the church to the building committee. She recommended they hire the firm of Rush, Endacott & Rush and make her former 22 year old student Bruce Goff the architect in charge of making her vision a reality. Contracts stipulated Adah would be in charge of all things artist inside and outside of the building. Adah spent an entire year studying Methodist church history in order to properly incorporate the appropriate symbolism through the art designs used for the church. In 1928, Adah established and headed the art department at the University of Tulsa. She received an honorary doctorate from the University in 1936. Tulsa art deco buildings: Boston Avenue Methodist Church, Adah Robinson Residence, Woodward Park Shakespeare Monument.

Leon Bishop Senter (1889-1965)

Leon Senter was the President of the State Board of Governors of Licensed Architects in Oklahoma when the licensing law went into effect. He was therefore issued License #1. At times he had Fredrick Kershner and Joseph Koberling working for his firm.

Tulsa art deco buildings: The Philcade Building, Tulsa Fire Alarm Building, Will Rogers High School, Tulsa University Skelly Stadium, Service Pipe Line Building

Joseph R Koberling Jr. (1900-1991)

Born in Budapest, Hungary, he was the son of architect Joseph Koberling Sr. who designed Tulsa's famous cave house. He designed the Medical & Dental Arts Building, Tulsa's first Art Deco building.
Tulsa art deco buildings: Will Rogers High School, Public Service Company Building, City Veterinary Clinic, J. R. McGay Residence, Medical Arts Building, Chamber of Commerce Building.

Frederick Vance Kershner (1904-1980)

Kershner graduated from Oklahoma A & M (Oklahoma State) in 1926 at which time he attended the Ecole des Beaux Arts in Fountainebleau, France for Fine Arts studies. He returned to Tulsa and along with Joseph Koberling, would design the Oklahoma Natural Gas Building. In 1935 he joined the firm of firm of Smith and Senter and designed the Tulsa Fire Alarm Building.
Tulsa art deco buildings: Tulsa Fire Alarm Building, Century Geophysical, Burtner Fleeger Residence, Nimitz Junior High School.

Bruce Alonzo Goff (1904-1982)

Bruce Goff was an architectural child prodigy that began work at Tulsa's Rush, Endacott and Rush firm at the age of 12. He graduated from Central High School in 1922 and was one of Adah Robinson's favorite art students. Later in 1925 he collaborated with Adah on the construction of the Boston Avenue Methodist Church and her personal studio/residence.

While designing the two side altars for Christ the King Church (1926) he met the artist Alfonso Iannelli who was designer of the stained glass windows. In 1934 he rejoined Iannelli in Chicago as a teacher at the Chicago Academy of Fine Arts. Being in Chicago also afforded Bruce the opportunity to meet and study the works of his childhood idols, Frank Lloyd Wright and Louis Sullivan. Goff emulated many of Wright's features in his work.

In 1947, Goff returned to Oklahoma as a professor at the University of Oklahoma. In 1948, he became Chairman of the Department of Architecture. While in Norman he designed several house. Most notable is the art deco styled Bavinger House, which is considered Goffs signature building. Bruce Goff designed sixty one Tulsa buildings between 1927 and 1931.

Goff is considered one of the most inventive and iconoclastic architects of the twentieth century. Goff had over 150 architectural designs built in fifteen states. His design's sensitivity to client needs, site, space, and material set him made him a unique architectural legend.

Bruce Goff was an architect on the following Tulsa art deco buildings: Boston Avenue Methodist Church, Adah Robinsons residence, Tulsa Club, The Riverside Studio, Guaranty Laundry and Midwest Equitable Meter Company.

Gone but not Lost

Tulsans are appreciative of the art deco style. They restore and maintain it when possible. Often they incorporate the old deco materials into newer buildings such as the Terra Cotta from the old Union Depot Bus Station (demolished in 1987) being restored and used in Tulsa's Emergency Medical Services Authority (EMSA) headquarters.

Tulsa's Old Municipal Airport entrance was re-constructed as an exhibit at the Tulsa Air and Space Museum (TASM). The Lobby of Tulsa Historical Society utilizes terra cotta from the Thomas Cadillac dealership that was demolished in 1997.

Route 66 Tulsa Experience

Where Route 66 Intersects Art Deco

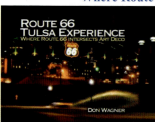

Only $15.99

During the development of Route 66, Tulsa experienced great success and wealth from the petroleum industry and constructed one of the country's top three cities for Art Deco buildings. Art Deco integrates with Route 66 throughout Tulsa. No city has been more of an integral part of Route 66's development and history than Tulsa.

Tulsa is truly engrossed in the tradition of "America's Main Street" and is investing heavily to ensure that tradition lasts for generations in the future. Find out about Tulsa's Route 66 history and future in Route 66 Tulsa Experience.

Route 66 Oklahoma Experience

**Only $19.99
(October 2010)**

No state has more miles of Route 66 than Oklahoma. Cyrus Avery, the "Father of Route 66" was from Tulsa Oklahoma and redirected the "Mother Road" through the state. See multiple Route 66 corridors through Oklahoma City and Tulsa to explore. See 66 traditions like Arcadia's Round Barn, Blue Whale, Totem Pole Park ,The Rock Café. See new attractions like the Route 66 Park, 2 Route 66 Museums and Pops. Route 66 cover in Oklahoma like never before.

Tulsa Trivia

So you think you know about Tulsa. See how well you do answering over 1600 Tulsa trivia questions on such categories as :

- History
- Geography
- Art Deco
- Route 66
- Buildings
- Local Sports
- Schools
- Tulsa Culture
- Entertainment
- Local Radio
- Attractions
- Local Television
- Business
- Movies & Theaters
- Diners & Bars
- Oil Industry

Only $15.99

Tulsa Picture Album

Tulsa Picture Album is a visual guide through Tulsa, by someone with 60 years experience living in the city. It is an excellent review of the city that shows others what a beautiful city is and what an interesting place it is to visit and live. It shows Tulsa's distinct districts, reflecting its diverse history that influenced its development including being the "Oil Capital of the World" and the birth place for Route 66.

Only $15.99

Additional Sources of Information
Work by the Tulsa Preservation commission was used to identify many Art Deco structures in this book. www.tulsapreservationcommission.org

Tulsa Art Deco by Tulsa Foundation for Architecture ,1961 was both a source and inspiration for this book. I strongly recommend this book to anyone interested in Art Deco architecture.

Here's to you Adah Robinson , by Jo Beth Harris. A great book about a remarkable woman.

Tulsa Historical Society www.tulsahistory.org

Tulsa Books
www.Tulsa-Books.Com
(918) 693-1198